Ou Light & Easy recipes

Copyright 2005, Gooseberry Patch
First Printing, December, 2005

All rights reserved. No part of this book may be reproduced or utilized in any form or by any means, electronic or mechanical, including photocopying and recording, or by any information storage and retrieval system, without permission in writing from the publisher. Printed in Korea.

Light Cooking Tips & Tricks

Make a few easy changes for healthy, tasty family meals...

- Eat more fruits and veggies! Fresh produce displays are bursting with delicious varieties to try...frozen and canned veggies are always handy in your cupboard and freezer.

- Reduced-fat dairy products like milk, sour cream, cream cheese and shredded cheese taste great...and are so easy to substitute in recipes.

- Olive oil and canola oil are higher in heart-healthy fats than other vegetable oils.

- Whole-grain pastas and flour add fiber to your diet...oats, brown rice and barley are excellent choices too. Sprinkle wheat germ or flax seed into baked goods for extra fiber and a nutty taste.

- Substitute margarine for butter, if you like. While "light" butters and margarines aren't meant for baking, it's easy to reduce fat in baked treats...just replace the oil in a recipe with an equal amount of applesauce.

- Try new sugar-substitute blends made especially for baking up sweet, golden, moist goodies with half the sugar. Be sure to check the package for how to measure correctly.

Before marinating chicken for grilling, pour some marinade into
a plastic squeeze bottle for easy basting...how clever!

Grilled Lemon-Herb Chicken   *Makes 4 servings*

4 T. lemon juice
2 T. dry white wine or fat-free
    chicken broth
1 T. olive oil
salt and lemon pepper to taste

2 T. fresh lemon thyme or
    rosemary, chopped
4 boneless, skinless chicken
    breasts

Whisk together all ingredients except chicken. Spray a grill or broiler pan with non-stick vegetable spray; preheat. Grill or broil chicken until juices run clear, brushing several times with lemon mixture.

For fuss-free veggies, lay them on heavy-duty aluminum foil,
dot with butter or olive oil and seal the foil. Place the package
on the grill for a few minutes, just until they're tender.

Chicken Italiano

Makes 4 servings

4 boneless, skinless chicken breasts
8-oz. bottle reduced-fat Italian salad dressing
2 c. bread crumbs

2 T. Italian seasoning
1 T. grated Parmesan cheese
1 T. dried parsley
1 clove garlic, finely minced

Place chicken in a large plastic zipping bag. Pour salad dressing over chicken; seal bag and refrigerate overnight. Combine bread crumbs with remaining ingredients in a shallow dish. Shake excess dressing off chicken; roll in bread crumb mixture. Arrange chicken in a baking pan sprayed with non-stick vegetable spray. Bake, uncovered, at 325 degrees for 45 minutes, or until juices run clear when pierced.

Before heating the grill, brush the rack with oil or use non-stick vegetable spray...it keeps foods from sticking and makes clean-up a breeze.

Teriyaki Chicken Breasts

Makes 4 servings

4 boneless, skinless chicken breasts
3 T. sugar or equivalent no-calorie sweetener
1/3 c. soy sauce
1/3 c. white wine or fat-free chicken broth
1/2 t. ground ginger
2 cloves garlic, minced

Lightly pound chicken with a meat mallet to flatten; place in a plastic zipping bag. Combine remaining ingredients and stir until sugar dissolves; pour over chicken. Seal bag and refrigerate for one to 2 hours, turning several times. Spray grill or broiler pan with non-stick vegetable spray; preheat. Discard marinade. Grill chicken for 3 to 5 minutes per side, until juices run clear.

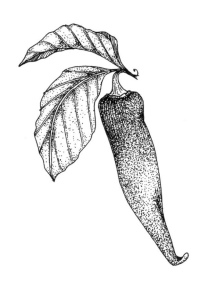

Soak wooden skewers in water for 30 minutes before adding
meat and veggies...skewers won't burn when grilled.

Hot & Spicy Ginger Chicken

Makes 4 servings

1/2 c. water
1/4 c. white vinegar
1/4 c. olive oil
1/2 c. onion, chopped
5 slices fresh ginger, peeled
2 dried chiles, crumbled

1 T. hot pepper sauce
1 t. dried thyme
1/2 t. allspice
1/2 t. pepper
1-1/2 lbs. boneless, skinless
    chicken breasts, cubed

Purée all ingredients except chicken in a blender; pour into a large bowl. Add chicken cubes, tossing gently; cover and refrigerate for 4 hours. Drain mixture into a small saucepan; bring to a boil, then transfer to a serving bowl for dipping. Arrange chicken cubes on 4 to 6 wooden skewers. Grill chicken for 5 minutes on each side, until juices run clear.

For extra-lean ground turkey or beef, pour meat into a colander after browning. Rinse with hot water...this washes away most of the remaining fat.

Hearty Turkey Chili

Makes 4 to 6 servings

1 lb. ground turkey
1 onion, chopped
1 c. celery, chopped
15-1/2 oz. can kidney beans,
    drained and rinsed
15-oz. can corn, drained
14-1/2 oz. can diced tomatoes

1 T. chili powder
1 t. salt
pepper to taste
Garnish: chopped onion,
    reduced-fat shredded
    Cheddar cheese, fat-free
    sour cream

Brown turkey, onion and celery together in a stockpot; drain well.
Stir in remaining ingredients; bring to a boil, reduce heat and simmer
for 25 to 30 minutes. Garnish individual servings as desired.

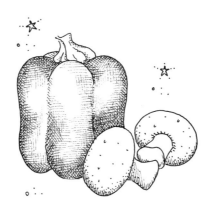

Trying to cut back? Set a pretty place for dinner with a lacy napkin,
a few blooms in a tiny vase and a salad plate instead of
a dinner plate. Your portions will seem bigger!

Turkey-Stuffed Peppers

Makes 8 servings

8 green peppers, tops removed
1 lb. ground turkey
1/3 c. onion, chopped
1 c. reduced-fat shredded mild
    Cheddar cheese, divided

1-1/2 c. croutons
2 tomatoes, chopped
1/2 t. Worcestershire sauce
salt to taste

Bring a large pot of water to a boil; add peppers and boil for 5 minutes.
Drain peppers well; arrange in a lightly greased shallow baking dish
and set aside. Brown turkey and onion together in a skillet over
medium heat; drain. Stir in 1/2 cup cheese, croutons, tomatoes and
Worcestershire sauce. Sprinkle salt inside peppers; fill peppers with
turkey mixture. Cover and bake at 350 degrees for 25 minutes.
Uncover and sprinkle with remaining cheese; bake an additional
5 to 10 minutes.

Good china and lit candles aren't just for holidays or special
celebrations...use them to brighten everyday meals!

Turkey Stroganoff

Makes 2 to 4 servings

3/4 lb. ground turkey
1 onion, diced
1 T. olive oil
2 cloves garlic, chopped
2 t. beef bouillon granules

4-oz. can sliced mushrooms, drained
2 c. fat-free sour cream
7-oz. pkg. yolk-free medium egg noodles, cooked

In a skillet over medium heat, brown together turkey and onion in oil, stirring in garlic, bouillon and mushrooms when partially done. Drain. Stir in sour cream; heat through without boiling. Arrange warm noodles on serving plates; spoon turkey mixture on top.

It's easy to get more veggies into your family's meals.
Keep frozen vegetable blends on hand to toss into
scrambled eggs, chicken noodle soup or even mac & cheese
for lunch with a veggie punch!

Rosemary Roasted Pork Loin *Makes 6 to 8 servings*

3-lb. boneless pork tenderloin	1 t. salt
2 t. dried rosemary	1 t. pepper
2 t. dry mustard	2 T. olive oil
1 t. ground ginger	6 cloves garlic, minced

Place tenderloin in an ungreased shallow roasting pan; set aside. Crush together seasonings in a mortar and pestle. Add oil and garlic to make a paste. Spread mixture over meat; let stand at room temperature for 30 to 45 minutes. Bake at 350 degrees for one to 1-1/2 hours. Let stand 15 to 20 minutes before slicing.

Today's
Special:

Get up and get going...a daily walk will do you a world of good!
Make your dog your personal trainer and go exploring
around your neighborhood or a nearby park.

Caraway Pork & Cabbage

Makes 3 to 4 servings

2 T. oil, divided
1 lb. boneless pork tenderloin,
    sliced into thin strips
1/2 head cabbage, shredded
1 onion, diced

1-1/2 c. fat-free chicken broth,
    divided
2 t. caraway seed
salt and pepper to taste
2 green peppers, sliced

Heat one tablespoon oil in a large skillet over medium heat. Sauté pork strips in oil until browned; remove from skillet and set aside. Add cabbage and remaining oil to skillet; sauté until wilted. Add onion; continue cooking until tender. Stir in 1/2 cup broth, caraway seed, salt and pepper; raise heat and simmer until most of the liquid has evaporated. Pour in remaining broth; return to a boil, then reduce to a simmer. Return pork to skillet; add peppers, cover and simmer until crisp-tender.

Salsa is flavorful, naturally fat-free and good on so many more foods than just tacos! Try a spoonful of salsa as a topper for grilled chicken, burgers, hot dogs or even baked potatoes...yum!

Beef Fajita Skewers

Makes 4 servings

1 lb. boneless beef top sirloin,
  sliced into strips
1 green pepper, quartered
1 red pepper, quartered
2 onions, thickly sliced
3 T. lime juice

1/3 c. reduced-fat Italian salad
  dressing
salt to taste
flour tortillas, warmed
Garnish: salsa

Thread beef strips evenly onto 4 wooden skewers; thread peppers and
onions alternately onto another 4 skewers. Combine lime juice and
salad dressing in a small bowl; brush beef and vegetables with
mixture. Grill skewers over hot coals, turning occasionally, allowing
7 to 9 minutes for beef and 12 to 15 minutes for vegetables. Add salt
to taste. Serve with tortillas and salsa, as desired.

Plan ahead for soups and stews that are practically fat-free.
Simmer soup the day before, refrigerate overnight and simply
lift off any fat that floats to the top.

Beefy Vegetable Soup

Makes 8 servings

1/2 lb. ground beef sirloin
1/2 c. onion, diced
4 to 5 14-1/2 oz. cans fat-free
    beef broth
2 c. water
4 carrots, peeled and diced
4 stalks celery, sliced
4 potatoes, peeled and diced
45-oz. can pinto beans, drained
    and rinsed

28-oz. can crushed tomatoes
14-oz. can kidney beans,
    drained and rinsed
1/2 T. dried parsley
1/2 T. dried basil
pepper to taste
1/2 of a 16-oz. pkg. whole-
    wheat thin spaghetti,
    uncooked

Brown ground sirloin and onion in a large soup pot over medium heat;
drain. Add remaining ingredients except spaghetti. Simmer until
vegetables are tender, about 30 minutes. Bring to a boil. Break
spaghetti into short lengths and add to soup. Cover and simmer an
additional 10 minutes until tender.

Leftover baked or grilled salmon makes a delicious light lunch!
The next day, just arrange a fillet on a bed of mixed greens
and drizzle with salad dressing.

Lemon-Parsley Salmon

Makes 6 to 8 servings

8 4-oz. salmon fillets
1/3 c. reduced-fat mayonnaise
2 T. sweet onion, diced

1 T. fresh parsley, chopped
2 t. lemon juice

Arrange salmon fillets in a 13"x9" baking pan that has been sprayed with non-stick vegetable spray; set aside. Combine remaining ingredients in a small bowl until smooth; spread evenly over each fillet. Bake at 425 degrees for 15 minutes, until fish flakes easily.

Brighten a dinner plate with edible fruit and veggie garnishes...try carrot curls, radish roses, pineapple spears or kiwi slices.

Skewered Sea Scallops

Makes 4 servings

2 T. lime juice
1 T. canola oil
1 clove garlic, pressed
1/2 t. ground cumin

1/8 t. cayenne pepper
1 lb. sea scallops
2 c. cherry tomatoes

Whisk together lime juice, oil, garlic and seasonings in a small bowl; set aside. Arrange scallops and tomatoes alternately on 4 to 6 wooden skewers and brush with lime juice mixture. Place skewers on a platter; cover and refrigerate for 30 minutes. Grill over hot coals for 5 to 7 minutes, basting frequently with mixture.

There's no better way to flavor foods than with fresh herbs.
Some tasty ones to try are rosemary, thyme, marjoram, chives
and basil. Grow pots of herbs on the kitchen windowsill or look
for freshly-cut bunches in the produce section.

Buttery Herb-Baked Fish

Makes 3 to 4 servings

1/2 c. butter or margarine
2/3 c. saltine crackers, crushed
1/4 c. grated Parmesan cheese
1/4 t. garlic powder

1/2 t. dried basil
1/2 t. dried oregano
1 lb. frozen fish fillets, thawed,
    separated and drained

Melt butter in a 13"x9" baking pan in 350-degree oven. Combine cracker crumbs, Parmesan and seasonings in a shallow dish; mix well. Dip fish fillets into melted butter and then into crumb mixture, coating well. Arrange fillets in baking pan. Place in center of oven and bake at 350 degrees for 25 to 30 minutes, or until fish flakes easily.

A big glass of water before dinner helps take the edge off
hunger. Keep a chilled pitcher of water in the fridge...dress it
up with slices of lemon or lime. So refreshing!

Foil-Wrapped Catch of the Day

Makes 2 servings

2 fillets haddock, flounder
   or sole
2 green onions, finely chopped
4 mushrooms, thinly sliced
1 c. zucchini, thinly sliced
1 c. carrots, peeled and thinly
   sliced

2 t. fresh chives, minced
4 t. lemon juice
1/2 t. dill weed
1/4 t. paprika
pepper to taste

Arrange each fish fillet in the center of a length of aluminum foil.
Top each fillet with half the remaining ingredients. Fold aluminum foil
over each fillet, sealing edges very tightly. Place packages on a baking
sheet; bake at 450 degrees for 15 to 20 minutes. Open packages
carefully, watching for escaping steam; fish is done when it flakes
easily and vegetables are tender.

Keeping the menu all veggie? Round off a veggie main dish
with special cheeses and breads...relax and enjoy.

Farmers' Market Stew

Makes 6 servings

1 eggplant, peeled and cubed
3 zucchini, thinly sliced
3 yellow squash, thinly sliced
2 onions, chopped
2 tomatoes, chopped
1 green pepper, chopped
1 clove garlic, minced

1 t. hot pepper sauce
2 T. olive oil
1 t. chili powder
1/2 t. curry powder
salt and pepper to taste
Optional: reduced-fat shredded
    mozzarella cheese

Combine all ingredients except cheese in a large kettle (no liquid
is needed). Cover and simmer over low heat for one hour, stirring
frequently. If desired, sprinkle individual portions with shredded cheese.

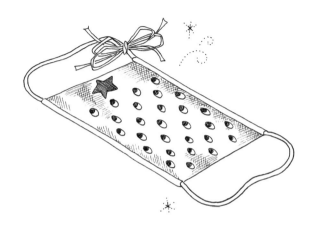

Non-stick vegetable spray is a great way to save both time and
fat calories when sautéing, stir-frying and baking. Just a spritz
keeps grilling meats juicy and frozen French fries tasty!
Look for olive oil and butter varieties for added flavor.

Zucchini Pizza

Makes 6 servings

1-1/4 lbs. zucchini, coarsely
    grated
2 eggs, beaten
8-oz. pkg. reduced-fat shredded
    mozzarella cheese, divided
1/2 c. grated Parmesan cheese

1/3 c. all-purpose flour
1 T. olive oil
1 c. spaghetti sauce
1 t. dried oregano
1/8 t. red pepper flakes

Press zucchini between paper towels to remove excess moisture.
Combine zucchini, eggs, one cup mozzarella, Parmesan and flour
in a medium bowl. Stir well; spread in a 13"x9" baking pan sprayed
with non-stick vegetable spray. Bake, uncovered, at 350 degrees for
20 to 25 minutes. Remove from oven; brush with oil. Broil pizza
5-1/2 inches from heat for 5 minutes. Remove from oven; spread with
spaghetti sauce. Sprinkle with remaining mozzarella, oregano and red
pepper flakes. Bake, uncovered, at 350 degrees for an additional
20 minutes. Cut into squares to serve.

Give whole-wheat pasta a try...it tastes great and contains
more fiber than regular pasta. The kids will never
know the difference!

Vegetable Lasagna

Makes 8 servings

10-oz. pkg. frozen spinach,
    thawed and drained
15-oz. container fat-free ricotta
    cheese
1 c. zucchini, thinly sliced
1 c. yellow squash, thinly sliced
1 c. carrots, peeled and thinly
    sliced

1 c. broccoli, chopped
8-oz. pkg. whole-wheat
    lasagna, uncooked
26-oz. jar marinara sauce
12-oz. pkg. reduced-fat sliced
    mozzarella cheese
1/2 c. grated Parmesan cheese

Mix spinach and ricotta cheese; set aside. Bring a large pot of water to a rolling boil; add vegetables and lasagna. Return to a boil and cook until tender, 5 to 7 minutes. Drain well. Spoon one-third of sauce into a greased 13"x9" baking pan; add a layer of lasagna, half the spinach mixture, vegetables and Parmesan cheese. Continue to layer with remaining ingredients, topping with sauce and mozzarella. Bake at 350 degrees for 30 minutes, until hot and bubbly.

No matter what looms ahead, if you can eat today, enjoy today,
mix good cheer with friends today, enjoy it and bless God for it.
-Henry Ward Beecher

Fresh Tomato-Basil Linguine *Makes 4 servings*

2-1/2 lbs. tomatoes, sliced
1-1/2 c. fresh basil, loosely
   packed
2 T. fresh parsley
3 cloves garlic, chopped

1/2 c. olive oil
salt and pepper to taste
16-oz. pkg. whole-wheat
   linguine, cooked

Combine all ingredients except pasta in a food processor until smooth.
Place hot cooked pasta in a large serving bowl; top with sauce. Toss
and serve immediately.

Stock up on pre-cut and peeled veggies like carrots,
onions and broccoli flowerets at the salad bar...they make
meal preparation a snap.

Veggie Grinders

4 whole-wheat sub buns, split
4 slices reduced-fat Swiss
   cheese
4 slices fat-free American
   cheese
1/4 c. reduced-fat Italian salad
   dressing

Garnish: leaf lettuce, sliced
   tomatoes, mushrooms,
   green peppers, green
   onions, olives
Optional: hot pepper slices,
   chopped fresh parsley

Lay sub buns cut-side up on a baking sheet. Arrange a Swiss cheese
slice on each top and an American cheese slice on each bottom. Bake
at 350 degrees just until cheese melts, about 10 minutes. Remove
from oven; layer bottoms with vegetable slices. Sprinkle vegetables
with salad dressing; garnish with hot pepper and parsley if desired.
Add bun tops; slice each sandwich in half and serve warm.

Bags of salad mix and coleslaw mix are real time-savers.
Keep opened bags crispy by storing in airtight containers or
plastic zipping bags...just be sure to press out all the air
before refrigerating.

Sunflower Slaw

1 head cabbage, shredded
5 carrots, peeled and shredded
1-1/2 c. pineapple cubes
3-1/2 oz. pkg. roasted
    sunflower kernels

3/4 c. reduced-fat mayonnaise
2-1/2 T. lemon juice
2-1/2 T. orange juice

Combine cabbage, carrots, pineapple and sunflower kernels in a large bowl; toss well and set aside. Combine remaining ingredients in a small bowl, blending well. Pour over cabbage mixture and toss to coat. Chill before serving.

Whip up some creamy Dijon-Parmesan salad dressing...low-fat
and delicious over fruit salad or grilled chicken. Combine one cup
buttermilk, one cup fat-free sour cream, 1/3 cup grated Parmesan
cheese, one tablespoon Dijon mustard, one teaspoon lemon juice
and 1/4 teaspoon pepper. Blend until smooth.

Melon Salad with Honey Dressing *Makes 4 servings*

1 cantaloupe, peeled, seeded
   and cubed
1 honeydew, peeled, seeded
   and cubed

3 T. lime juice
2 T. balsamic vinegar
3 T. honey
6-oz. pkg. mixed greens

Combine melon cubes in a large bowl; set aside. In a small bowl, whisk together lime juice, vinegar and honey, blending well. Pour over melon and toss. Arrange greens on salad plates. Using a slotted spoon, remove melon from bowl and arrange over greens. Drizzle with dressing from bowl.

Good to know...the darker the salad greens, the healthier they are for you. Try spinach, romaine, spring mix...if iceberg lettuce is more to your taste, try a mix of iceberg and darker greens.

Tomato-Red Pepper Salad

Makes 4 to 6 servings

2 red peppers, halved
1 red onion, sliced
6 tomatoes, cubed
1/4 c. olive oil

1 T. basil or chive vinegar
1 T. lemon juice
1 T. fresh basil, chopped
1 T. fresh mint, chopped

Arrange peppers and onion slices on a baking sheet; broil for about 5 minutes, until pepper skins start to pucker. Let cool slightly; peel peppers and cut into strips. Place peppers, onion and tomatoes in a bowl; set aside. Whisk oil, vinegar and lemon juice together in a small bowl. Stir in basil and mint; toss dressing with vegetables. Cover and refrigerate for at least 2 hours.

Fresh veggies don't need to be fussy. A simple vegetable
antipasto means forgetting about plates and forks
with a tasty pick-up-and-munch snack.

Broccoli & Cauliflower Salad *Makes 10 to 12 servings*

1 head broccoli, chopped
1 head cauliflower, chopped
3 stalks celery, diced
1 onion, chopped
8-oz. container fat-free sour
    cream

3/4 c. reduced-fat mayonnaise
1 t. garlic powder
1/2 t. salt
10 slices turkey bacon, crisply
    cooked and crumbled

Combine vegetables in a large bowl; toss to mix and set aside. In a small bowl, mix sour cream, mayonnaise, garlic powder and salt. Pour over vegetables. Add bacon; toss to mix well. Chill before serving.

Serve up fruit salads in old-fashioned glass compotes so
all the bright colors show through. Top with a dollop of fat-free
whipped topping for a special treat!

7-Fruit Salad

Makes 8 to 10 servings

1/2 c. lime juice
1/2 c. water
1/2 c. sugar or equivalent
    no-calorie sweetener
2 peaches, peeled and thinly
    sliced
1 banana, thinly sliced

1 honeydew melon, halved
    and seeded
1 pt. blueberries
1 pt. strawberries, sliced
1 c. red seedless grapes, halved
1 kiwi, peeled and diced

In a medium bowl, whisk together lime juice, water and sugar. Stir well until sugar is dissolved. Add peaches and banana; toss to coat. Scoop honeydew with a melon baller. Combine melon balls with remaining fruit in a large bowl; stir in peach mixture. Cover and refrigerate for one hour.

Fat-free vinaigrette is so fresh-tasting on salad greens.
Just fill a cruet bottle with 1/2 cup herb-flavored vinegar,
2 tablespoons water, one tablespoon Dijon mustard, 2 teaspoons
Worcestershire sauce, 4 teaspoons sugar or sweetener,
2 pressed garlic cloves and a dash of pepper...shake and enjoy!

54

Great Greek Salad

10 c. mixed greens
8-oz. container crumbled
    feta cheese
3-1/4 oz. can sliced black
    olives, drained
1 cucumber, diced
1 red onion, thinly sliced
1 tomato, chopped

1/4 c. olive oil
1/4 c. lemon juice
2 t. sugar or equivalent
    no-calorie sweetener
2 cloves garlic, pressed
Italian seasoning and
    pepper to taste

Toss together greens, cheese and vegetables in a large salad bowl;
set aside. Combine remaining ingredients in a jar with a tight-fitting
lid; shake well. Pour dressing over salad; toss to coat.

Plant a vegetable garden...digging, planting and weeding
are great exercise and the fresh air and sunshine will do you
good. No room for a garden? Look for home-grown
veggies at a nearby farmers' market.

Cottage Salad

1 c. broccoli flowerets
1 c. cauliflower flowerets
1 to 2 T. water
1/2 c. carrot, peeled and
    shredded
1 green onion, finely chopped
1/4 c. radishes, sliced

1/4 c. green pepper, sliced
12-oz. container low-fat cottage
    cheese
1/4 t. dill weed
1/8 t. garlic powder
1/8 t. dry mustard

Combine broccoli, cauliflower and water in a saucepan; heat over medium heat until crisp-tender. Drain and let cool. Combine remaining ingredients in a large bowl. Mix lightly and stir in cooled vegetables. Cover and refrigerate until chilled.

Keep wooden salad bowls looking their best...wash them with warm, soapy water and dry, then rub inside and out with wax paper. The wax from the paper will keep the surface of the bowl sealed.

Spinach-Orange Tossed Salad

Makes 6 servings

10 c. baby spinach
3 oranges, peeled and sliced
1 red onion, sliced and
    separated into rings
1/3 c. orange juice

1/3 c. cider vinegar
1/3 c. olive oil
1/4 c. fresh cilantro, chopped
2 T. sugar or equivalent
    no-calorie sweetener

In a large bowl, combine spinach, orange slices and onion rings; set aside. Combine remaining ingredients in a jar with a tight-fitting lid. Shake well to combine and pour over spinach mixture; toss.

For a no-fuss, low-fat meal, spoon grilled veggies onto
a softened tortilla and roll up...delicious!

Grilled Vegetable Salad

Makes 6 servings

1 to 2 carrots, peeled and
  thickly sliced
1 red pepper, cubed
1 yellow pepper, cubed
2 zucchini, thickly sliced
2 yellow squash, thickly sliced
1 onion, thickly sliced

1/3 c. balsamic vinegar
2 T. olive oil
2 shallots, finely chopped
1 t. Italian seasoning
1/4 t. salt
1/4 t. pepper
1-1/2 t. molasses

Combine vegetables in a large bowl; set aside. Whisk together
remaining ingredients and pour over vegetables; toss to coat. Let
stand 30 minutes, stirring occasionally. Drain, reserving vinegar
mixture. Arrange vegetables in a grill basket that has been sprayed
with non-stick vegetable spray. Grill, covered, over medium to hot
coals, 15 to 20 minutes, turning occasionally. Return vegetables to
reserved vinegar mixture; tossing gently. Serve warm or cover and
refrigerate overnight.

Make a crunchy, fresh salad fast with no dishes to wash!
Toss lettuce, veggies and any other toppers in a one-gallon
plastic zipping bag.

Herbed Rotini Salad

Makes 4 servings

12-oz. pkg. whole-wheat
   rotini pasta, uncooked
1/2 red pepper, cut into strips
1/2 green pepper, cut into strips
1/2 yellow pepper, cut into
   strips

3-oz. pkg. crumbled feta cheese
1/3 c. sliced black olives
1 to 1-1/2 T. olive oil
1/4 c. fresh basil, chopped
1/4 t. red pepper flakes

Prepare rotini according to package directions, cooking just until tender. Rinse with cold water; drain well. Combine rotini with remaining ingredients in a large bowl. Toss to coat; cover and chill overnight.

When freezing leftover diced peppers, sweet onions, corn or
fresh herbs, add a little olive oil to the freezer bag and shake.
The oil will help keep pieces separate and fresher too. They'll be
ready to drop into sauces, salsas and salads!

A to Z Veggie Delight

2 c. asparagus, sliced into
   2-inch lengths
2 c. zucchini, peeled and diced

2 T. butter or margarine
1 c. sliced mushrooms
1/8 t. dill weed

In a skillet over medium heat, sauté asparagus and zucchini in butter until crisp-tender. Add mushrooms and dill weed, stirring until mushrooms are golden.

Pick up a bunch of flowers on your next grocery shopping trip!
Even the simplest bouquet of daisies tucked into a glass pitcher
adds cheer to the dinner table.

Lemony Herbed Asparagus

Makes 4 servings

1 lb. asparagus spears, trimmed
1 T. olive oil
1/8 t. dried basil

1/8 t. dried oregano
1/8 t. pepper
1 t. lemon juice

Cook asparagus in water until tender; drain and remove to a serving platter. Combine oil, herbs and pepper in a small saucepan. Cook and stir over medium heat until heated through. Remove from heat; stir in lemon juice. Drizzle over asparagus.

For a little extra zing, add a squeeze of lemon or lime
to any salad or veggie dish.

Zingy Marinated Tomatoes

Makes 6 servings

6 tomatoes, thickly sliced
1/4 c. green onion, thinly sliced
1/4 c. fresh parsley, minced
2 T. fresh thyme, minced
1 clove garlic, minced

1 t. salt
1/4 t. pepper
2/3 c. olive oil
1/4 c. red wine vinegar

Arrange tomato slices on a shallow plate or dish; set aside. In a small bowl, combine onion, herbs, garlic, salt and pepper; sprinkle mixture over tomatoes. Shake together oil and vinegar in a jar with a tightly fitted lid; pour over tomatoes. Cover and refrigerate for several hours or overnight, spooning dressing over tomatoes occasionally. Drain tomatoes before serving, if desired.

For a low-calorie supper, turn a veggie dish into a flavorful supper. Make the servings larger than usual and add a crisp salad alongside.

Zucchini Skillet Medley

Makes 3 to 4 servings

1 to 2 T. olive oil
3/4 c. celery, sliced
1/2 c. onion, sliced
1 clove garlic, minced
1 lb. zucchini, sliced
2 tomatoes, diced
1 carrot, peeled and shredded

1/2 green pepper, diced
8-oz. can tomato sauce
2 t. mustard
1/4 t. dried basil
1/4 t. salt
1/8 t. pepper

Heat oil in a skillet over medium heat; sauté celery, onion and garlic until tender. Add remaining vegetables and sauté an additional 10 minutes, until tender. Stir in tomato sauce, mustard and seasonings; simmer for 5 minutes. Serve warm or chilled.

Make your own salt-free herbal seasoning! Fill a shaker-top jar with 5 teaspoons onion powder, a tablespoon each of garlic powder, paprika and dry mustard, a teaspoon of dried thyme and 1/2 teaspoon each of celery seed and cayenne pepper. Keep tightly sealed. Great on veggies and potatoes!

Oven-Baked "Fries"

Makes 2 to 4 servings

2 baking potatoes, cut into
  1/2-inch wedges
2 t. olive oil

2 t. paprika
salt and pepper to taste

Brush potato wedges with oil; arrange on a baking sheet sprayed
with non-stick vegetable oil. Sprinkle with paprika, salt and pepper
to taste. Bake at 425 degrees for 15 to 20 minutes, until tender
and golden.

Take the children to a pick-your-own farm or local farmers'
market. Later they'll be much more willing to eat
"their" fruits & vegetables.

Smoky Green Beans

Makes 4 servings

4 slices hickory-smoked turkey
    bacon, diced
1 sweet onion, diced

24-oz. can green beans
8-oz. can tomato sauce

In a large skillet over medium-low heat, sauté bacon and onion
together for 15 minutes, stirring often. Add green beans; stir in tomato
sauce. Cover and simmer over low heat for one hour.

Even the simplest dinner is made special by candlelight. Light one
tall pillar candle or a grouping of tiny tealights for a warm glow.

Honey-Dill Carrots

Makes 4 servings

4 carrots, peeled and sliced   1/4 to 1/2 t. dill weed
1-1/2 T. honey

Barely cover carrots with water in a medium saucepan. Simmer over
medium heat for 10 to 12 minutes, just until tender. Drain. Add honey
and dill weed; stir until coated.

Invite friends over for a casual dinner...let everyone help by bringing a dish. What a wonderful way to try new recipes!

Braised Red Cabbage

Makes 8 servings

3 slices turkey bacon, diced
1 onion, diced
1 head red cabbage, shredded
1 red apple, peeled, cored and
    diced

1 t. cider vinegar
1 t. sugar or equivalent
    no-calorie sweetener
salt to taste

Crisply cook bacon in a large saucepan over medium heat; set bacon aside, reserving drippings in pan. Sauté onion in drippings until tender; add cabbage, apple, bacon and enough water to cover. Simmer over medium-high heat until cabbage is tender. Drain well; stir in vinegar, sugar and salt.

Be sure to get the most flavor from dried herbs...simply rub
them together between your fingers to release the oils.

Toasted Barley Pilaf

Makes 8 servings

1 T. olive oil
1 c. pearl barley, uncooked
1/2 c. onion, chopped
1 c. sliced mushrooms

2 c. fat-free chicken broth
1/2 t. dried marjoram
salt and pepper to taste

Heat oil in a heavy saucepan over medium heat. Add barley and sauté for 10 minutes, stirring frequently, until golden. Add onion and cook for 2 minutes; add mushrooms and cook an additional 2 minutes, until soft. Add broth and marjoram; bring to a boil. Reduce heat, cover and simmer for 45 minutes, until barley is tender and broth is absorbed. Stir in salt and pepper to taste.

Pack leftover veggie dishes into small containers for next day's lunch. Add a little sliced lean meat or some reduced-fat cheese cubes and you've got a delicious, healthy lunch all set to go.

Green Beans in Garlic Butter

Makes 6 servings

1 c. fat-free chicken broth
salt and pepper to taste
2 lbs. green beans, trimmed
    and halved

4 cloves garlic, thinly sliced
1/4 c. butter or margarine,
    melted

Bring chicken broth, salt and pepper to a boil in a large saucepan. Add green beans and heat until tender, stirring often. Drain green beans and place in a serving bowl; set aside. Sauté garlic in butter in a small skillet until golden; pour over green beans, tossing to coat. Serve warm.

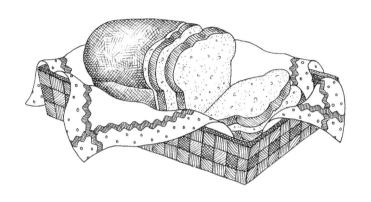

Slow down at meals...you'll eat less! It takes about 20 minutes after you start eating for your stomach to know it's full. Share the day's events with your family, listen to calming music or just think pleasant thoughts!

Whole-Wheat Quick Bread

Makes one loaf

2 c. whole-wheat flour
1/2 c. soy flour
1 t. baking soda
1 t. baking powder
1/4 c. wheat germ

1/4 c. fat-free powdered milk
1/2 t. salt
1-1/2 c. fat-free milk
1/2 c. honey or molasses

Combine flours, baking soda, baking powder, wheat germ, powdered milk and salt in a large bowl; mix well. Add milk and honey or molasses, stirring until moistened. Spoon into a 9"x5" loaf pan sprayed with non-stick vegetable spray; let stand while oven preheats. Bake at 350 degrees for 45 to 50 minutes, until a toothpick inserted in center comes out clean. Let cool in pan for 10 minutes; turn out onto a cooling rack to finish cooling.

Try sweetened, dried cranberries in place of raisins in your next recipe...a sweet-tart surprise that's good for you too.

Coffee Can Molasses Bread

Makes 2 loaves

2 c. whole-wheat flour
1/2 c. cornmeal
2 t. baking soda
1/2 t. salt
2 c. buttermilk

1/2 c. molasses
1/2 c. raisins
1/2 c. dried apples, finely
    chopped

Combine all ingredients in a large bowl. Grease and flour 2, one-pound coffee cans; spoon batter equally into cans. Let stand for 30 minutes. Bake at 350 degrees for 50 to 55 minutes, or until tops are golden and a knife inserted in center comes out clean. Remove from oven; let cool for 15 minutes. Turn loaves out of cans and let cool completely.

Add nutrition and subtract fat from muffins, quick breads and brownies...it's a snap. Just replace any oil with the same amount of applesauce, puréed prunes or mashed pumpkin.

Oatmeal-Apple Muffins

Makes one dozen

1 c. quick-cooking oats,
    uncooked
3/4 c. fat-free milk
Optional: 1/2 c. raisins
1-1/4 c. all-purpose flour
2 t. baking powder
1/2 t. salt
1/2 t. cinnamon

1 egg
1/4 c. canola oil
1/2 c. brown sugar, packed,
    or equivalent no-calorie
    sweetener
1/2 c. apple, peeled, cored
    and diced

Combine oats and milk in a small bowl; let stand for several minutes. Cover raisins with hot water to plump, if using; drain. Combine flour, baking powder, salt and cinnamon in a medium bowl; mix well and set aside. Beat together egg, oil and brown sugar until blended. Stir in oat mixture; add to flour mixture. Blend in apple and raisins, if using. Spoon into muffin cups sprayed with non-stick vegetable spray, filling three-quarters full. Bake at 400 degrees for 15 to 20 minutes.

Nuts and seeds add fiber plus crunch and flavor too! Stir chopped almonds or walnuts into cereals and quick breads...sprinkle sunflower kernels over salads.

Banana-Walnut Muffins

Makes one dozen

1-3/4 c. all-purpose flour
1/2 c. sugar or equivalent
    no-calorie sweetener
1 t. baking powder
1/2 t. baking soda
1/2 t. nutmeg

1/2 t. cinnamon
1/2 t. salt
1 c. banana, mashed
1/2 c. applesauce
2 eggs
1/2 c. chopped walnuts

Combine flour, sugar, baking powder, baking soda, spices and salt in a large bowl. Mix well; make a well in the center and set aside. Blend together banana, applesauce and eggs in a medium bowl; add to dry ingredients. Stir just until moistened; stir in nuts. Spoon into 12 muffin cups sprayed with non-stick vegetable spray. Bake at 350 degrees for 20 minutes. Serve warm.

If extra muffins are too tempting, freeze them! Muffins freeze
well wrapped in heavy aluminum foil...just pop 'em in the oven at
300 degrees, still wrapped, for 12 to 15 minutes to warm.

Cinnamon Muffins

Makes one dozen

1-1/2 c. whole-wheat flour
1-1/2 t. baking powder
1/2 t. baking soda
1-1/2 t. cinnamon
1/4 t. salt
1 egg

1 c. buttermilk
1/2 c. frozen apple juice
   concentrate, thawed
3 T. applesauce
2 T. canola oil

In a large bowl, stir together flour, baking powder, baking soda, cinnamon and salt. Make a well in the center; set aside. In a separate bowl, combine remaining ingredients; add to flour mixture and stir until moistened. Spoon into muffin cups sprayed with non-stick vegetable spray, filling three-quarters full. Bake at 400 degrees for 20 minutes.

Make your own tortilla or pita chips for scooping up healthy low-calorie dips! Cut flour tortillas or pita rounds into wedges, brush lightly with olive oil and sprinkle with salt or dried herbs if you like. Bake at 350 degrees until crisp. Yummy!

Texas Tomato Salsa

Makes 4 cups

2 14-1/2 oz. cans stewed
   tomatoes
1/2 c. onion, finely chopped
1/4 c. diced green chiles
3 T. fresh cilantro, chopped

1-1/2 T. lime juice
1 t. salt
garlic salt and pepper to taste
baked tortilla chips

Combine all ingredients except tortilla chips in a food processor. Blend to desired smoothness. Chill. Serve as a dip with tortilla chips or use as a topping for grilled chicken, burgers, etc.

Keep ready-to-eat veggies like baby carrots, celery sticks, cherry tomatoes and broccoli flowerets in the fridge...handy for snacking anytime!

Fresh Herb & Garlic Dip

Makes 2 cups

1 c. fat-free sour cream
1 c. reduced-fat mayonnaise
2 T. fresh parsley, chopped
2 T. fresh chives, chopped
2 T. fresh garlic chives, chopped

1 T. fresh thyme, chopped
1 T. fresh rosemary, chopped
1 clove garlic, pressed
sliced vegetables

Combine sour cream, mayonnaise, herbs and garlic in a medium bowl; mix well. Cover and refrigerate overnight. Serve with assorted vegetables for dipping.

Try red pepper strips, endive leaves, cucumber slices and snow peas as fresh and tasty alternatives to potato chips for scooping up creamy dips!

So-Good Spinach Dip

Makes about 3 cups

12-oz. container low-fat cottage
  cheese
1 c. reduced-fat mayonnaise
1 T. lemon juice
1.4-oz. env. vegetable soup mix
1 T. onion, grated

10-oz. pkg. frozen spinach,
  thawed and drained
8-oz. can water chestnuts,
  drained and chopped
reduced-fat snack crackers or
  sliced vegetables

Spoon cottage cheese into a blender; blend until smooth. Spoon into
a bowl; combine with mayonnaise, lemon juice, soup mix, onion,
spinach and water chestnuts. Mix well and chill. Serve with crackers
or vegetables for dipping.

Try using fat-free cream cheese or ricotta cheese in your favorite dip recipe instead of regular cream cheese. Just as creamy and good but much better for you!

Snappy Shrimp Dip

Makes 1-1/2 cups

8-oz. pkg. fat-free cream
    cheese, softened
4-1/2 oz. can tiny shrimp,
    drained
1 T. prepared horseradish

1 T. reduced-fat mayonnaise
1/8 t. Worcestershire sauce
1/8 t. lemon juice
1/2 c. cocktail sauce
reduced-fat snack crackers

Combine all ingredients except cocktail sauce and crackers in a
medium bowl; blend well. Chill for one hour or more. At serving time,
shape into a ball and set on a serving dish. Spoon cocktail sauce
around ball. Serve with crackers for dipping.

Beans add flavor and fiber to hearty recipes...try mashed cannellini, kidney, black or pinto beans in place of, or in addition to, ground beef.

Cheesy Mexican Dip

Makes 8 cups

2 15-oz. cans turkey chili
      with beans
16-oz. container fat-free
   sour cream
12-oz. jar salsa

1-1/2 c. reduced-fat shredded
   Cheddar cheese
1 T. taco seasoning mix
baked tortilla chips

Layer ingredients, except chips, in order given on a microwave-safe pie plate or serving plate. Cover; microwave on high setting for 5 minutes, or until cheese is melted. Serve with tortilla chips for dipping.

Need a snack to tide the kids over until dinner? Head to the
pantry and mix up mini pretzels, crunchy cereal squares,
raisins and nuts...toss in a few candy-coated chocolates
for fun and let them enjoy!

Fruity Yogurt Smoothie   *Makes 2 servings*

2 6-oz. containers fat-free
    fruit-flavored yogurt
1/2 c. peach or strawberries,
    sliced

1 banana, sliced
1 c. orange or pineapple juice
6 ice cubes

Combine all ingredients in a blender; blend until smooth. Pour into
glasses and serve immediately.

Iced tea is a refreshing beverage anytime! Simply place
2 family-size teabags in a 2-quart pitcher of cold water.
Refrigerate overnight to brew. Serve sweetened or
unsweetened, as you like.

Pink Party Lemonade

Makes 10 servings

6-oz. jar maraschino cherries,
    drained
12-oz. container frozen pink
    lemonade concentrate,
    thawed

1-ltr. bottle sugar-free
    lemon-lime soda, chilled
ice cubes

Place a cherry in each section of an ice cube tray; fill with water and freeze. Prepare lemonade in a large pitcher, adding water as directed on package. At serving time, stir in soda and serve over ice cubes.

A cup of hot tea is a soothing, relaxing way to begin or end the day. Try fragrant chamomile or orange spice tea...they need little or no sweetener.

Fat-Free Cappuccino Mix

Makes 10 servings

6 T. plus 2 t. instant espresso
   coffee powder
1-1/4 c. fat-free powdered
   non-dairy creamer

1/2 c. plus 2 t. sugar or
   no-calorie sweetener
3 T. plus 1 t. baking cocoa
1 T. vanilla powder

Combine all ingredients, stirring well. Store in an airtight container.
For each serving, add 3/4 cup boiling water to 1/4 cup mix; stir well.

Create a cheerful table runner. Lay Gerbera daisies down the center of the table...arrange votive candles and colorful red, green and yellow peppers around them.

"Egg" Nog

1-oz. pkg. instant sugar-free
    vanilla pudding mix
1/3 c. sugar or equivalent
    no-calorie sweetener

1/2 gal. fat-free milk
2 t. vanilla extract
1/2 t. nutmeg

Mix all ingredients well in a large bowl or pitcher; chill.

Easy lunch box dippers! Wrap up sliced apples and send along
a cup of reduced-fat peanut butter for dipping. Or try packing
salsa or reduced-fat ranch salad dressing for dipping
celery and carrot sticks.

Mile-High Strawberry Pie   *Makes 6 to 8 servings*

1-1/2 c. plus 1 T. water, divided
1/4 c. cornstarch
.3-oz. pkg. sugar-free
    strawberry gelatin mix
4 c. strawberries, sliced

9-inch reduced-fat graham
    cracker crust
8-oz. container fat-free frozen
    whipped topping, thawed

Stir together one tablespoon water and cornstarch in a cup until
smooth; set aside. Bring remaining water to a boil in a saucepan; stir
in cornstarch mixture until thick. Add gelatin mix, stirring well; fold in
berries. Pour into crust; refrigerate until set. Top with whipped topping.

Happiness being a dessert so sweet,
May life give you more than you can ever eat.

–Irish toast

Berry Good Lemon Torte

Makes 10 to 12 servings

.3-oz. pkg. sugar-free lemon
   gelatin mix
1/2 c. boiling water
1/3 c. frozen lemonade
   concentrate, thawed
1 T. sugar or equivalent
   no-calorie sweetener

12-oz. can fat-free evaporated
   milk
1 angel food cake, cubed
Garnish: 2 c. raspberries

In a large bowl, dissolve gelatin mix in boiling water. Stir in lemonade, sugar and evaporated milk. Cover and chill for one to 1-1/2 hours. Beat chilled mixture with an electric mixer on high setting for 5 to 6 minutes, until fluffy. Arrange cake cubes in an 8" round springform pan sprayed with non-stick vegetable spray. Pour gelatin mixture over cake; chill for 4 hours. At serving time, remove sides of springform pan. Cut into wedges; spoon raspberries over top.

Make dessert a grand finale....serve it
on sweet vintage flowered china plates.

Chocolatey P.B. Pie

Makes 6 to 8 servings

2 c. fat-free milk
2 1.4-oz. pkgs. instant sugar-
    free chocolate pudding mix
1/2 c. reduced-fat creamy
    peanut butter

9-inch reduced-fat graham
    cracker crust
8-oz. container fat-free frozen
    whipped topping, thawed
Optional: baking cocoa

Combine milk and pudding mix in a medium bowl. Whisk together until thickened; stir in peanut butter. Spoon into crust; spread with whipped topping. If desired, sprinkle with baking cocoa. Chill for several hours until firm.

Look for new sugar-substitute blends that work perfectly
in baking, while cutting down on sugar...there's even a
brown sugar variety!

Crunchy Peanut Butter Bars

Makes one dozen

1/2 c. honey
1/2 c. brown sugar, packed, or
    equivalent sugar substitute
1 c. reduced-fat crunchy peanut
    butter

4 c. whole-grain rice flake cereal
1 c. dried fruit, chopped

In a heavy saucepan over medium heat, bring honey and brown sugar to a boil; remove from heat. Add peanut butter; stir until melted. Fold in cereal and fruit. Press mixture into an 11"x9" baking pan sprayed with non-stick vegetable spray. While still warm, cut into bars with a pizza cutter. Let cool.

Creamy fat-free vanilla yogurt makes a delicious topping for
fresh strawberries, nectarines and blueberries.

Very Cherry Trifle

Makes 10 to 12 servings

1 angel food cake, cubed
1.4-oz. pkg. instant sugar-free
    vanilla pudding mix
1-1/2 c. fat-free milk
8-oz. container fat-free sour
    cream

20-oz. can sugar-free cherry
    pie filling
8-oz. container fat-free frozen
    whipped topping, thawed

Place cake cubes in the bottom of a clear glass serving bowl; set aside. Combine pudding mix, milk and sour cream in a mixing bowl. Beat until thickened, about 2 minutes; let stand for 3 to 5 minutes. Spoon pudding mixture over cake; spread pie filling over pudding, then spread topping over pie filling. Refrigerate until serving time.

Baked apples are delicious and oh-so easy. Set cored apples in a baking pan and spoon a little brown sugar substitute, cinnamon and red cinnamon candies into the centers. Cover with plastic wrap and microwave on high for 4 to 5 minutes. Mmm!

Fresh Honeydew Sorbet

Makes 6 servings

1 honeydew melon, peeled,
    seeded and cubed
1/4 c. sugar or equivalent sugar
    substitute

1/4 c. lime juice

Purée melon cubes in a food processor or blender. Combine with sugar and lime juice in a mixing bowl. Stir well until sugar is thoroughly dissolved. Spoon into an ice cream maker and freeze according to manufacturer's directions. Keep frozen.

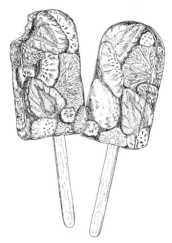

For easiest-ever fruit pops, simply thread big chunks of ripe fruit like watermelon, bananas, strawberries, kiwi and peaches onto wooden skewers. Serve right away or freeze 'til solid.

My Favorite Cheesecake

Makes 10 to 12 servings

8-oz. pkg. fat-free cream
    cheese, softened
5 eggs
2-3/4 c. sugar or equivalent
    sugar substitute, divided

1/4 t. almond extract
2 T. vanilla extract, divided
2 c. fat-free sour cream
Garnish: 1 c. berries or sliced
    peaches

In a mixing bowl, combine cream cheese, eggs, 2 cups sugar, almond extract and one tablespoon vanilla. Beat until smooth with an electric mixer on medium speed. Pour into a 9" round springform pan sprayed with non-stick vegetable spray. Bake at 350 degrees for one hour and 10 minutes. Mix together sour cream, remaining sugar and remaining vanilla; pour over hot cake. Bake at 350 degrees for an additional 10 to 15 minutes. Chill. At serving time, remove sides of springform pan. Cut into wedges and garnish with fruit.

INDEX

INDEX

How Did Gooseberry Patch Get Started?

Gooseberry Patch started in 1984 one day over the backyard fence in Delaware, Ohio. We were next-door neighbors who shared a love of collecting antiques, gardening and country decorating. Though neither of us had any experience (Jo Ann was a first-grade school teacher and Vickie, a flight attendant & legal secretary), we decided to try our hands at the mail-order business. Since we both had young children, this was perfect for us. We could work from our kitchen tables and keep an eye on the kids too! As our children grew, so did our "little" business. We moved into our own building in the country and filled the shelves to the brim with kitchenware, candles, gourmet goodies, enamelware, bowls and our very own line of cookbooks, calendars and organizers! We're so glad you're a part of our **Gooseberry Patch** family!

For a free copy of our **Gooseberry Patch**
catalog, write us, call us or visit us online at:

Gooseberry Patch
600 London Rd.
★ P.O. Box 190 ★
Delaware, OH 43015

1·800·854·6673
www.gooseberrypatch.com